STEPHANIDES BROTHERS'

GREEK MYTHOLOGY

SERIES B: GODS AND MEN   **No. 7**

DEUCALION'S FLOOD

retold by MENELAOS STEPHANIDES
illustrated by YANNIS STEPHANIDES

translation BRUCE WALTER

SIGMA PUBLICATIONS
20, MAVROMIHALI ST., TEL. 36.07.667, FAX: 36.38.941
GR-106 80 ATHENS, GREECE

DEUCALION'S FLOOD

4th edition revised 1994

ISBN 960-425-021-3

THE FIVE AGES OF MAN

Our distant ancestors, who lived long, long ago in the very earliest days of Greek civilization, said that the immortal gods had created the human race not once, but five times.

The first race of all, they believed, was happy and god-like, so they named them the Golden Generation, and they called the times they lived in the Golden Age. Their life, they said, was one continual round of pleasures. They lived in perfect harmony with one another, free from cares and sorrows and untouched by war or natural disasters. They did not know what it meant to be tired, sick or in pain. Not even old age could wither them and they remained young and strong to the end. And when death finally did come to them, after many long and happy years, it stole upon them like a sweet sleep. As long as they lived they had all they could desire, for the earth was a true paradise and gave its rich fruits in abundance. Their placid flocks grazed peacefully in the green meadows, they lacked nothing and never knew hunger or want.

THE GOLDEN GENERATION

Although in the end they were all destroyed in punishment for the dreadful sins of the titan Cronus, the god who then ruled the world, when they died they became immortal spirits. They floated invisible over the face of the earth, punishing evil, repaying good deeds and upholding justice. This reward was given to them after their deaths by Zeus, when he in his turn became ruler of the world.

THE SILVER GENERATION

The Silver Generation was the next to inhabit the earth. How unlike the men of the Golden Age these newcomers were! Weak and foolish, they were incapable of managing their own affairs, let alone of helping others. For the first hundred years of their lives they were like helpless children in need of a mother's care, though even that was lacking often enough. And when they did finally grow up, their adult life was short, for they could not distinguish between good and evil, between what might help them and what might do them harm; and so they led lives filled with pain and sorrow. They had no appetite for work and no love for one another. They lived on what they could take by force and often ended up by killing one another in bloody quarrels. They disobeyed the immortal gods and never offered them sacrifices.

Angered by their evil deeds and by their lack of respect for the gods, Zeus sent them all to the joyless black depths of Hades, and by this punishment the Age of Silver was brought to an end.

Then Zeus, son of Cronus, created the third generation, the men of

THE BRONZE GENERATION

the Age of Bronze, or the sons of Pelasgus as they were sometimes called, after the name of one of their great kings.

The Age of Bronze bred men of mighty stature and invincible strength. They were terrifying in appearance and fearless warriors. They were clad in bronze and always ready to do battle. Their weapons were forged from bronze, and their dazzling armour was beaten from the same metal. Their tools were of bronze, and they even lived in brazen houses, for in those days man had not yet learned the use of iron. They did not plough the land, but lived by hunting and gathering wild fruit, and war was their constant companion. Yet although their mighty strength and stature were the gift of the gods, and not of their own creating, in the end they grew arrogant and swollen with foolish pride. Their looks became harsh and overbearing, and their hearts as hard as stone.

ΠΕΡΣΕΑΣ

ΙΑΣΟΝΑΣ

ΗΡΑΚΛΗΣ

THE HEROIC GENERATION

Yet however fearsome and strong they may have been, they did not escape their fate. Enraged by their insolence, Zeus despatched them all to the dark kingdom of the shades. And thus they, too, were cut off from the bright light of the sun.

Now a fourth generation came into the world, made glorious by Heracles, Theseus, Jason, Achilles and the whole great army of fearless heroes of Greek mythology. It was their deeds which gave the fourth generation its name: the Heroic Age.

Nobler and juster than their predecessors, the men of the Heroic Age were as fair as the gods themselves. The immortals often came down from Olympus and moved among them, sharing their joys and their sorrows. Many of their kings and the founders of their noble lines were fathered by some god, and the Olympians stood by them and protected them. Great and powerful cities rose and flourished during this period. The most renowned of them all

ΘΗΣΕΑΣ ΑΧΙΛΛΕΑΣ ΟΔΥΣΣΕΑΣ

was gilded Mycenae — for we have now reached the glorious age of Mycenaean civilization.

But nothing is eternal. A time came when even the generation of heroes was brought low. Countless warriors fell at the seven gates of Thebes, giving battle for the riches of King Oedipus, and more still died in the ten-year struggle before the walls of Troy — warriors who had sailed from every city of Greece in their galleys for the sake of fair Helen, daughter of Zeus. And when they had all been killed, Mycenae lost and Tiryns, Cnossus, Pylos and Iolchus and many another fair city, then great Zeus raised them up and took them to live far from the eyes of men in the Fortunate Isles, far, far away in the boundless ocean, in the most distant reaches of the world. In that remote place the Heroic Generation lead a life free from all pain and bitterness. There the earth yields its crops three times in a year, and its fruits are as sweet as honey.

5

THE IRON GENERATION

With the passing of the heroes the mythical ages came to an end. The fifth generation which Zeus brought into the world was the human race, the workers of iron who still inhabit our abundant earth.

Life was difficult for this fifth generation. They had to work hard to survive, and their lives were beset with trials and problems. Even the gods seemed not to love them, for they withdrew to Olympus and from there showered disasters and bitter disappointments upon men's heads. Of course, they also dealt them out a few joys among all these sorrows, but the evil always outweighed the good and overshadowed their lives.

The men of the fifth generation lived with the memory of the race that had gone before them. The mythical era left a rich cultural heritage to its successors. Minstrels, poets and story-tellers went from city to city and from village to village recounting the heroic deeds of the lost generation at festivals, fairs and weddings. One of these was Homer, the blind ballad-singer who became the greatest poet of all times. Later, the immortal tragedies of Sophocles, Euripides and Aeschylus were to be performed in every city in Greece. And their themes were always borrowed from that unforgettable fourth generation, the mythical race of heroes.

These memories have came down to us over the centuries and are fresh even today — for there is one thing we should never forget, that Greek mythology deals above all with the exploits of the fourth generation, and when it died out, mythology came to an end.

But before we begin to speak of this age of renown we should look back at the one that came before it, to learn how the Age of Bronze vanished from the earth, and how the fourth generation of men came into the world.

PROMETHEUS
THE PROTECTOR OF MANKIND

As we have said before, mighty Zeus did not love the men of the third age, because they had grown proud and overbearing. For that reason he finally decided to overthrow them. It was not a sudden decision, however, and many things happened before Zeus finally made up his mind to take action. To take up the story from the beginning, it must be said that the men of the Age of Bronze had not always been bad. On the contrary, they had meant well at first and praised and worshipped the gods. Yet life was hard in those early days. Men had not yet learned to make fire and lived in the woods in rough shelters, caves or hollow trees.

And so they would have continued to live had it not been for Prometheus the titan, son of Iapetus. No other god loved mankind as he did. Prometheus dedicated his life to a great and noble goal: to stand at the side of mortal men and help them achieve a better life. He never counted the cost, although he knew beforehand how dearly he would eventually pay for the great love he felt towards mankind.

But, as he always said, "Nothing good and beautiful can be achieved without sacrifice."

**FIRE:
A GIFT
FROM THE GODS**

His first good deed was to give men fire. He took it from the forge of Hephaestus and, holding it aloft like a lighted torch which banished the darkness, he brought it, running, to his friend man.

"A gift from the gods!" men exclaimed; and with the burning brand Prometheus had given them they lit undying fires everywhere to give themselves light and heat, to roast their food and to offer sacrifices to the gods. Yet this was not enough. Next Prometheus showed them how to work with fire. Soon they had built their first furnaces and began to smelt ore. They learned how to work bronze, silver and gold. From the bronze they made their tools, their household utensils, their weapons and everything else that they needed. They loved this metal, and wore bronze armour, and from then on became known as the bronze generation.

Prometheus' help did not stop here, however. Next he taught men how to tame the beasts of the field. It was thanks to him that mortals first learned to ride horses, drive the first chariots and cross the seas in the first ships. Prometheus even taught them to fight against disease. It was from him they learned to boil herbs over the fire to prepare medicines, and thus death was no longer quite the threat it had been till then. Prometheus even taught men to interpret oracles, to avoid ill-fortune and to overcome their difficulties. With his help new horizons opened for mankind. The gift of fire filled their minds with light, their hearts with warmth and their bodies with new vigour

MAN LEARNS ARTS AND CRAFTS

and strength. Now there was but one difference between gods and men: they were mortal while the gods lived for ever.

These developments did not meet with the approval of Zeus. For you see, the men of the Age of Bronze were mighty of stature, and once they had mastered the use of fire they were many times stronger than before. Now the ruler of gods and men began to fear them.

PROMETHEUS QUARRELS WITH ZEUS

"It is all the fault of Prometheus," Zeus complained. "He is the one who gave them fire and helped them to become equal with the gods." The problem left him no rest, and in the end he began to heap misfortunes on mankind so that they would lose the power the son of Iapetus had given them.

But Prometheus boldly resisted Zeus' efforts.

"I cannot see mankind plunged into pain and sorrow," he said, and so he secretly continued to offer help and bring them new joys.

When the lord of the world heard what Prometheus had been doing, he was beside himself with rage.

"Tread softly, son of Iapetus," he threatened, waving his fist. "Defy me once more and I shall make you wish you had never been born."

"Learn this, son of Cronus," Prometheus replied. "I am not to be cowed by threats or broken by torture. You have forgotten the battles we once fought together and now you seek to frighten me into obedience. Do you not remember the battle of the Titans, where we struggled to save not only the gods, but man, too, from tyranny? I do not say that evil-doers should go

9

unpunished, especially when they are powerful and lord it over whole cities or peoples. But why make all mankind suffer when they are only trying to improve themselves?''

With every such exchange of words the enmity between Zeus and Prometheus grew more bitter.

And at Sicyon things came to a head.

THE MEETING AT SICYON

Gods and mortals had gathered there together to decide which parts of the animals that men sacrificed should be offered to the gods and which should be kept by men. A great ox had been made ready for the ceremony. Prometheus was asked to divide it into two portions, and Zeus to decide which of them was to belong to the immortals and which to men.

Naturally, Zeus had no intention of giving away the best parts to mere mortals. Not that the gods had any need of the meat from the sacrifices, for they ate ambrosia and drank nectar, whose taste was sweet beyond men's imagining. What pleased the gods was the savoury smells which rose from the altar fires, and not the meat itself. Zeus, however, did not wish to do mankind any favours and he had already made up his mind: all the good meat would go to the gods and man would get nothing but the skin, the entrails and the bones.

Now Prometheus knew what Zeus had in mind, so he decided what he

must do: he would trick the ruler of gods and men.

First he cut up the ox, picked out all the good pieces and heaped them on a great platter. Then he covered them all with the bloodied skin of the animal.

Next he filled another platter with the bones and carefully covered them with shiny white fat so that not a single bone could be seen.

When Prometheus had finished, he took the two platters and presented them to Zeus who stood waiting to give judgement, flanked on his right by all the gods of Olympus and on his left by the mortals, each side equally impatient to see which of the two he would choose.

As soon as the ruler of gods and men saw the platter draped with the blood-spattered hide, an expression of disgust crossed his face and he turned away his eyes. Next his glance fell on the second platter, and at the thought of the good meat which must lie beneath that gleaming white fat his mouth began to water.

Turning to Prometheus he said: ''You may be the most intelligent of the gods, O son of Iapetus, but in this case you have divided most unfairly. So much the better. You have made my choice an easy one and I shall have no difficulty in deciding which portion should belong to the immortal gods.''

''Choose as you will, mighty Zeus,'' replied Prometheus. ''Your decision will be binding on gods and men alike.''

PROMETHEUS TRICKS ZEUS

Then Zeus pointed to the dish which gleamed with fat and said in a stern voice: "From now on this is the portion which shall belong to the gods; and that" — pointing to the other dish but not even deigning to look at it — "shall be the portion which belongs to men. That is my decision and nothing can ever change it!"

This last phrase had hardly escaped his lips when his face darkened. As if a suspicion had suddenly crossed his mind, he plunged his hands into the first dish, pushed the covering of fat aside — and exploded with rage. It was unthinkable! How could the lord of the world be fooled like this? Now mortal men would eat the sacrificial meat and for the immortal gods there would be nothing but the bones! And he himself had made the choice. What humiliation! However, the portions had been shared out now and nobody, not even Zeus himself, had the right to change them.

But there was something else he could do: he could withdraw the gift of the gods which Prometheus had offered mankind. He could take back their fire from heaven and deprive them of heat and light.

ZEUS TAKES BACK THE GIFT OF FIRE

12

PROMETHEUS STEALS BACK THE FIRE FROM OLYMPUS

"We shall see if they like their meat uncooked," said Zeus to himself. "Now perhaps they will not think their crafty friend Prometheus has done them such a good turn, after all."

And that is just what Zeus did. He took back the gift of fire and hid it high on lofty Olympus, warning Prometheus with these words:

"As for you, son of Iapetus, beware of my wrath, for you know how harsh I am when I wish to punish."

But Prometheus was never one to be ruled by caution, and there was no power on earth that could stop him from helping the human race. And so, the very next day, he secretly brought the fire back down from Olympus, hidden in a hollow reed, and gave it once more to mankind. And from that day on, men have always cooked and eaten the meat of their sacrifices and offered only the white bones to the gods on their fragrant altars.

This time, however, Zeus' anger knew no bounds. A fearful punishment awaited Prometheus for stealing the gift of fire and taking it back to men. But first the lord of the world intended to punish mankind, and to do this he hatched a secret plan.

Zeus ordered Hephaestus, the blacksmith of the gods, to make him a woman out of clay. He told him to make her as beautiful as a goddess, to give her voice and movement, and to fill her eyes with divine enchantment.

So Hephaestus took earth and water and carried out his father's orders with wonderful skill.

The lord of the earth was delighted when he saw the result of Hephaestus' labours. It was just what he needed.

"I intend her as a gift for mankind," Zeus told the other Olympians, and they ran to deck her with gifts.

PANDORA

The goddess Athena wove her splendid gowns, brighter than sunbeams. The Three Graces decked her with lovely, gleaming jewellery. The Hours crowned her with a wreath of fragrant, snow-white flowers. The goddess of love, Aphrodite, bestowed irresistible charm upon her, and all the other gods and goddesses offered her some gift which would embellish her beauty and grace. For this reason the young woman was named Pandora, which means in Greek "all the gifts".

Endowed with so much charm and beauty, Pandora could have been a wonderful gift for mankind; but Zeus took care that it should be otherwise. He gave secret instructions to his son Hermes, and in obedience to his father's commands the crafty god taught her to speak sweetly but falsely, and gave her a sly and treacherous character.

Then Zeus ordered Hermes to take the girl as a gift for Epimetheus, Prometheus' brother who lived on earth among mortals. Unfortunately, the two brothers bore little resemblance to each other, for Epimetheus was not only slow-witted but weak-willed. Prometheus had often warned him never to accept any gifts from Zeus if he wanted to keep out of harm's way, but as soon as Epimetheus set eyes on Pandora's ravishing beauty he completely forgot his brother's advice and welcomed her with open arms. By the time he remembered Prometheus' warning it was too late, for he had already taken

Pandora, the gift of Zeus, as his bride.

"Now I must be on my guard," he said to himself, thinking of a certain jar which stood in his house, a jar which Prometheus had carefully stoppered.

"Take care, Epimetheus," his brother had told him, "and make sure that this jar is never opened. For if it is, all manner of evils will be loosed upon the world." And from then on, Epimetheus had not only lost all desire to open the jar, but even to approach it.

Imagine Epimetheus' horror, then, when he found Pandora examining it curiously.

"Keep away from that jar, Pandora," he warned. "Prometheus gave instructions that it should never be opened. Take care, lest some great evil befall us all."

"Come now, why should I wish to open it," Pandora replied lightly. Yet in spite of her words, she could not drag her eyes from the intriguing object. Pandora's curiosity was aroused by most things that she saw, but above all by that jar, so carefully sealed and stoppered. And from the moment she was told to keep her hands off it, she was seized by such curiosity that she could not get a moment's rest.

"What can there be inside that jar and why am I not allowed to open it?" Again and again she asked herself this question until one day her inquisi-

15

EVIL SPREADS OVER THE EARTH

tiveness overcame her and, hardly able to wait until her husband had left the house, she rushed to the jar and opened it.

The moment she did so she uttered a piercing scream of horror, for from out of the jar swarmed a horde of hideous monsters: Evil, Hunger, Hate and Sickness, Revenge, Madness and a host of kindred spirits. A terrible fear seized Pandora when she saw all these horrors spreading over the earth and, not knowing what else to do, she plucked up what courage was left to her, seized the stopper and sealed the jar once more. But in so doing she shut in the only spirit that had not yet emerged from its prison — and this was the spirit of Hope. And so everything came to pass exactly as Zeus had planned.

Thus all manner of evils were loosed upon the world, settling like a pestilence on city and village alike, drifting like a foul mist into every household and turning the life of men into a succession of bitter woes.

Prometheus watched all this in helpless grief, his heart as heavy as lead. Yet Zeus in his wrath had even worse in store for mankind, and Prometheus would be forced to look upon the worst catastrophe that could befall them: their utter destruction.

T H E   F L O O D

When Pandora opened the jar and set free so many evils to prey upon the world, men grew wicked and cruel and ceased to respect the gods. It was then that Zeus finally decided to wipe them out. However, he needed some pretext for doing this, and the opportunity was given him by Lycaon, king of Arcadia, and his fifty sons.

Before the earth was overrun by evil, Lycaon, son of Pelasgus, was not only a good man but a worthy king, and there was no more faithful worshipper of Zeus among all the rulers of Greece. He built the first city in Greece, Lycosaura, and dedicated it to Zeus. He raised an imposing temple to him, a place of pilgrimage where the ruler of gods and men was worshipped in the manner that befitted him. He even founded athletic contests, the Lycaia, in homage to Zeus. They were the first such games in Greece.

Yet although the games were held in honour and praise of Zeus, it was precisely over these that the lord of the world found an excuse to destroy mankind.

The Lycaia were Panhellenic games. Every two years, that is, athletes and visitors came from all over Greece and were received with great hospitality.

17

**THE WORSHIP
OF XENIAS ZEUS**

Lycaon even put his own palace at the disposal of these visitors.

Hospitality was so highly regarded in those days that the athletic contests were combined with a festival in tribute to Xenias Zeus —"Zeus who welcomes guests". For they all believed that it was he who had laid down the sacred rules of hospitality.

But since that accursed day when Pandora had opened the jar and evil had spread over the world, Lycosaura had forgotten what hospitality meant. No one treated strangers kindly now, and so it came about that Lycaon, who had once honoured and worshipped Zeus above all men, now offered him the most deadly insult. And as you may have guessed, the incident occurred at those very games which were supposed to be held in Zeus' honour.

Athletes and visitors from every region thronged the streets of Lycosaura, for the Lycaian games were to begin next day. Now, however, no one was willing to take them into their homes as they had once done, and so the strangers wandered here and there like lost sheep and could find nowhere to sleep but in the streets and public squares.

Among the visitors was Zeus, disguised as an ordinary mortal. He wanted to see for himself the games and festival which were to be held in his name. But now he found every door barred against him and no one willing to give him food or shelter. In the end he decided to seek hospitality at the royal palace.

The stranger's commanding height and majestic appearance should have been enough to tell Lycaon who it was who stood before him. But no. Instead of this he cried out in fury:

"I have had enough of you foreigners. Why don't you sleep in the woods instead of dirtying our town?"

"The forests are for the wild beasts," replied Zeus, and at his words the steps of the palace were bathed in blinding light.

All those who were present, except Lycaon and his sons, knew by that sign that he who stood before them was none other than Zeus himself, and they fell on their knees and worshipped him.

"We do not worship strangers in the land of Pelasgus!" shrieked Lycaon

LYCAON REFUSES HOSPITALITY

in fury. "Bow the knee to your king, not to some foreigner!"

Then an old man stepped forward from the crowd and said in a stern voice:

"True, great king, we do not pay homage to strangers in this place, but in the past the sons of Pelasgus always worshipped Xenias Zeus and offered hospitality to every stranger that entered our gates. Now, however, we cast them out, and I fear that some great evil will befall our city and yourself. Receive this man we took for a stranger, for he has shown that he is no mere mortal but Zeus himself. Honour him as befits the ruler of the world, and prepare a splendid feast for him."

"Enough, old man," replied Lycaon, "I will receive this stranger. But do not presume to offer me advice on how I should do so, for that is mine to decide."

With these curt words Lycaon granted the old man's plea. He had no intention of honouring Zeus, however. His aim was to humiliate him.

And what a method he chose!

He ordered his sons to cook Zeus the most revolting meal that could possibly be imagined — and they served him up a mixture of animal and human flesh!

LYCAON TRIES TO HUMILIATE HIS GUEST

Of course, Zeus immediately realized what kind of dish had been set before him, and roared out in anger:

"So this is Lycaon! How dare he insult the ruler of the world so shamelessly!" No, Zeus would certainly not tolerate such treatment any longer! Beside himself with rage, he overturned the table and burned Lycaon's palace to the ground with a thunderbolt.

"And now it is you who shall go and live in the forest," he told Lycaon and his sons, flinging back their own words in their faces. And as he spoke they were transformed into the wild and ravenous beasts which have ever since been known in Greek as "lycoi", but which in English are called wolves.

Howling hideously, the beasts fled up into the dense forest behind the palace, up to Mount Lycaion, as it was afterwards called in their memory.

But Zeus' anger was not appeased by this punishment alone.

"So this is the famous human race!" he shouted in his fury. "Now let Prometheus look at them and admire their works! I shall not leave a single one of them on the earth. They shall perish, the guilty and the innocent alike. I will destroy them for all eternity, and he who loves them so shall be forced to look on before punishment falls on him, too — a greater punishment than god or man has ever suffered."

**THE TERRIBLE
WRATH OF ZEUS**

These were Zeus' words. Yet who had sent Pandora to earth? Who was responsible for the evils which now plagued the world? Who was to blame for the sorry state to which mankind had been reduced? Zeus considered none of these things as he took his decision: he would drown the human race in a mighty flood, and along with it every living creature upon the earth.

ZEUS AND THE WET SOUTH WIND

Standing before Lycaon's upturned table, he called the wet South wind to his side and bid it journey far out to where the titan Oceanus stretches wide and boundless, and there to gather cloud upon heavy cloud, bursting with the waters of mighty Oceanus, and then, blowing hard, to drive them quickly back to the mountains and the plains of the world.

Soon, heavy black clouds covered the whole earth. On and on they came until the entire sky was one vast expanse of black and all nature was clouded over.

Suddenly, sky and earth alike were lit up by a dazzling flash, and an ominous clap of thunder shook the whole world, echoing and re-echoing like

a harbinger of doom. There followed a deadly silence, heavy with fear. Then suddenly disaster struck. Amid a frightful turmoil of lightning and thunderclaps there began a downpour which seemed like a thousand waterfalls tumbling from the heavens. Down teemed the rain the clouds had gathered from the boundless ocean, in an inexhaustible and endless deluge.

Soon water covered the plains and the heights were flooded, yet the cataclysm continued unabated until all nature was one vast sea from horizon to horizon and even the high mountains were inundated. Now only lofty Olympus and the twin peaks of Parnassus still showed above the waters.

Where men had once tilled the fields fish now swam, and where man's flocks had once grazed schools of dolphins now sported. By rights, not a single human being should have survived the catastrophe. And yet it was not so. For once more Prometheus had thwarted Zeus' plans and saved the human race from total destruction.

Prometheus had a son, Deucalion, who was king of Phthiotis, and he had

PROMETHEUS SAVES THE WORLD

warned him of the impending flood and told him what he must do to save himself and his family.

As soon as he had received his instructions, Deucalion set to work. Hundreds of venerable oaks and straight and lofty cypress trees fell to the blow of his axe. For Deucalion was building an ark, a great vessel which would hold not only his family but a host of animals as well.

With the eager and untiring help of his wife, Pyrrha, and their children, Deucalion's work went forward briskly. The keel was carved from thick tree-trunks, the ribs slotted into it and the decks nailed on with wooden pegs. The seams were carefully caulked with pitch. Finally the roof was added, and that, too, was given a good coating of tar.

When all was ready, the animals began to go into the ark. They all arrived and went on board of their own accord, one male and one female of every

beast and bird in the world, from the proud lion to the crawling snake. They
offered one another no harm but went quietly to their appointed places as the
wise titan Prometheus had ordained.

DEUCALION'S ARK

With the help of Pyrrha and their children, Deucalion stocked the ark with
sufficient food to last them all, man and beast, for many days.

By the time all was ready the skies were dark with clouds, so Deucalion
ordered his wife and children to get on board without delay, and when they
had done so, he and his eldest son, Hellen, mounted the gangplank and
pulled it up behind them. It was clear that the weather was not going to wait,
and hardly had they made the hatches fast than the storm broke.

Soon the rising waters had lifted the ark from the earth. For nine days and
nine nights it drifted at the mercy of the tempest while Pyrrha and Deucalion
listened anxiously to the drumming of the seemingly endless rain. But on the

THE ARK COMES TO REST ON PARNASSUS

morning of the tenth day a sudden bump told them that the ark had found land once more. Deucalion ran to open a window. The rain had stopped, but a sheet of water stretched to the horizon in all directions, save for a little islet crowned by twin peaks where the ark had come to rest.

Deucalion knew the place.

"We are on the summit of Mount Parnassus," he exclaimed. "I believe the worst is over, but before we go ashore we must make sure the weather is not going to turn stormy again." Then he released a dove. In those days everybody knew that these birds have an unerring instinct for the weather, and so if it returned in alarm, it would mean that the storm was about to break once more and they should not leave the safety of the ark. But the dove perched at the open window for a moment, looked around at the weather and then flew joyfully to the mountain peak.

When he saw this, Deucalion put all the animals ashore and then stepped out onto dry land himself, followed by Pyrrha and their children.

Thus Prometheus saved the human race and all life was not washed from the face of the earth.

Now though it was believed in Greece that Deucalion's ark came to land on the slopes of Mount Parnassus, the Greeks of southern Italy said that the waves had carried the ark as far as their lands, and that it had finally come to rest on Mount Etna. In the eastern lands, on the other hand, another version of the myth prevailed, especially in the years following Alexander the Great's conquests. In those parts it was believed that the wind carried Deucalion's ark to the cedar-clad summit of Mount Lebanon, and until the coming of Christianity, the spot where the ark was believed to have come to rest was a place of pilgrimage throughout the East, so widespread was the myth of Deucalion and his ark in those far-off days.

But let us return to Deucalion, still huddled with his family near the mountain-top. Their first act on coming ashore had been to pray to Hera, wife of Zeus. They were still afraid to offer up their prayers to Zeus himself lest he fly into an even greater rage and blast them all with a bolt of lightning. Only Hera could calm him and soften his anger.

"Great queen of the skies," said Deucalion and Pyrrha, "look what evil has befallen the world. Tell Zeus to make the waters withdraw, and we shall be grateful to you for ever."

Hardly had they spoken when the mountain split asunder at their very feet and a bottomless gulf opened which began to swallow the waters with a great roar. Soon the boundless seas which had surrounded them were gone, and the mountains and plains were visible once again. Then the great rift closed. Where it had been, however, a crack remained in the earth, and over this spot Deucalion and Pyrrha built a temple to the goddess Hera. Then, having

THE MOUNTAIN IS RENT ASUNDER

**DESOLATION
AND DESTRUCTION**

offered up their thanks for her help, they loaded their few belongings on an animal and made their way down to the plains.

Not a soul could be seen anywhere. Desolation and decay surrounded them: ruined houses, uprooted trees, boulders and mud lay all around.

With heavy hearts they drew to a halt before the river Cephissus.

"We are the only ones who were saved," said Deucalion. "Come, let us build an altar and give thanks to almighty Zeus for granting us our lives."

When they had done this, and begged Zeus to help them, the god Hermes appeared, sent by the ruler of the world himself. And this is what he told them:

"Mighty Zeus was so pleased when he heard you offering up your thanks that he sent me to tell you that you may ask what you will of him, and he gives his word that your wish will be granted, whatever it may be."

"We would like the earth to be filled with people once again," replied the couple in unison.

Then Hermes hastened back to Olympus, and when Zeus heard what they had requested he sat in thought for a while and then finally said:

"So let it be. I am no longer angry with men. Now the time has come for Prometheus to pay." And to show how seriously he meant these words, he sent Themis herself, the goddess of law, to instruct Deucalion and Pyrrha.

She told them: "If you throw behind you the bones of your great mother, everything you have asked for shall be granted."

But Deucalion and Pyrrha did not have the same mother, for they were man and wife, not brother and sister, and for a while they were at a loss. Then, suddenly, Deucalion's face lit up. He had grasped the meaning that lay behind Themis' words and he cried:

"Olympian Zeus means that we should throw behind us the bones of Mother Earth, for it is she who is the great mother of us all."

"Yes, she is the mother of all things," replied Pyrrha, "and these pebbles are her bones."

"FILL THE EARTH WITH PEOPLE ONCE AGAIN"

THE EARTH IS REPEOPLED

Then they both stooped and picked up the stones that lay on the river bank and began to throw them back over their shoulders.

Immediately they did so, the stones that Deucalion threw became men, and those thrown by Pyrrha turned into women.

Thus the earth was filled with people once again, and thus it is that the ancient words for 'stone' and 'people' are almost the same.

And so the fourth generation of men came into the world.

Deucalion had many children by Pyrrha, and their descendants were all the renowned heroes of Greek mythology.

By their mighty deeds they brought glory to the generation which so justly bears their name: the Heroic Age; and however much the lord of the world may have hated Prometheus, fate so ruled that in the veins of that glorious breed of heroes Prometheus' blood should flow: for all the Greeks are said to spring from Hellen, son of Deucalion and grandson of Prometheus. And that is why the Greeks are also called the Hellenes.

Hellen succeeded to his father's throne and ruled in Phthiotis. He had three sons: Aeolus, Dorus and Xuthus. From Aeolus the Aeolians are de-

scended, from Dorus the Dorians, and from the sons of Xuthus, Ion and Achaeus, sprang the Ionians and the Achaeans.

Thus, so mythology would have us believe, the four races which make up the people of Greece were not only descended from the progeny of Prometheus, but even took their names.

Yet Zeus' hatred for Prometheus was not quenched by the waters of the flood. His wrath had been turned aside from man only to be directed even more fiercely against the proud titan. Now Zeus could no longer wait to punish Prometheus for daring to go against his will and for giving the gift of fire to the human race.

Prometheus knew that he would not escape the harsh punishment Zeus was preparing for him, and so he went secretly to find Athena and speak with her. Knowing how much the blue-eyed goddess loved mankind he told her:

PROMETHEUS HANDS ON HIS TASK TO ATHENA

"A terrible fate awaits me, Athena. I shall be bound with unbreakable chains and suffer horrible tortures for all eternity. However, it is not this which I fear most, but that mankind should be left without a helper."

"The sufferings you are doomed to bear are enough for you. Do not torture yourself over man's fate as well," replied Athena in a determined voice. "I will do all that you bid me and more."

Then Prometheus sat with the goddess and taught her architecture, astronomy, mathematics, shipbuilding, metalworking, medicine and many other arts so that she in her turn would be able to teach them to mankind.

"Perhaps it is better this way," said Prometheus when he was through. "Zeus loves you dearly, and he will not stand in your way. Besides, you know how to win him over, and I certainly do not."

"Never fear, brave titan, replied Athena. "I shall not fail you. And now, be of good courage."

Truly, of all the immortals Athena was the only one who could carry on the work of Prometheus. Her determination to succeed gave new strength to the great friend of mankind. His mind set at rest, he surveyed the green and fertile earth and imagined it as it would become, made more beautiful still by the work of man. Happiness filled his soul, and in a fearless voice he said:

"Now let Zeus do his worst to me. I am ready."

SOME ANSWERS TO POSSIBLE QUERIES

To those of our readers, young or old, whose reading of this mythology series may have prompted certain questions, we would like to say the following:

It is possible that you may have read the same myth elsewhere and noticed significant differences. This does not necessarily mean that one version is right and the other wrong. In their retelling, myths came to differ widely from place to place and from age to age and as a result several versions are now extant. In this work, we decided to give one version only, choosing either that most widely accepted, or the one we felt to have the most value. Working by the same criteria we have often added materials taken from other sources to round out a myth.

Another frequent cause of bewilderment are the contradictions generally encountered in mythology. For example, in one myth Zeus may be depicted as kind and fair, and in another tyrannical and unjust. Even Homer does much the same thing in the Iliad. At one point he has Thersites, a common soldier, lashing Agamemnon himself with the tongue of truth, while at another we see him crying like a child beneath the blows of Odysseus' gilded sceptre. These apparent contradictions must be accepted at face value, for it must not be forgotten that while sceptred monarchs had the right to command, the story-teller's lyre was in the hands of the common people, and clashes were inevitable. It is significant that while rulers are depicted as being the equals of Ares in power and daring, the singer-poets did not create a single myth in which the god of war emerges victorious, but many in which he suffers defeat and humiliation.

As for the illustrations, we believe that a picture should speak for itself. Nevertheless, we should like to say a few words about them.

We had to choose between two schools of thought. According to the one —and this is a line taken by many illustrators— we would have been obliged to remain faithful to the classical originals, chiefly vase-paintings, working in two dimensions, without perspective and with sparing use of colour. The other approach dictated that we use a modern style, and this we have preferred — but with one important prerequisite: that the picture, like the text, must itself be mythology. Thus, while keeping to the classical line, we have added a few elements of perspective where this seemed absolutely necessary. In one respect, however, we felt that we must have absolute freedom, and that was in the colouring. In our opinion, it was precisely the bright colours we have used which would give our work the fairytale air which the myths have to the modern reader's eye. For the ancients, in contrast, mythology was religion. For them the gods were real and not mythical beings. To us mythology is something else — a collection of wise and charming stories which shine like a bright fabric of the imagination from out of the depths of the centuries. It is for this reason that we have tried to illustrate this series with colour alone, or rather, by weaving harmonious contrasts of colour, but never forgetting that our theme is Greek mythology.